The BOYS' Annual 2009

Buster Books

CONTENTS

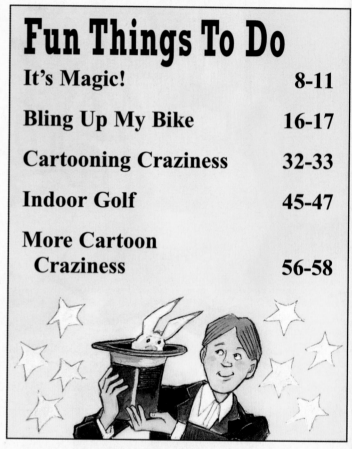

Things To Make

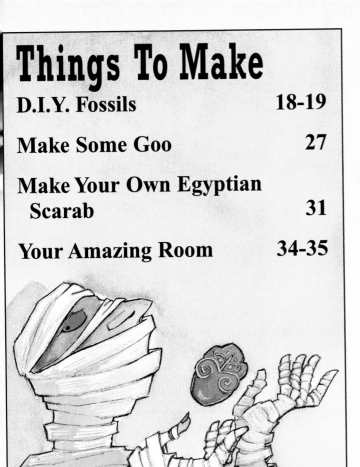

Quizzes & Puzzles

Interesting Facts

Joke Time

Answers

IT'S MAGIC!

Do you ever watch open-mouthed while a magician performs mind-blowing tricks? Well, here's your chance to learn a few tricks to perform yourself.

THE CLEVEREST CARD TRICK EVER!

For this trick, you will ask a friend to pick a playing card without telling you which one it is. Then, amazingly, you will read his mind and tell him which card he has chosen – magic!

You will need: 21 cards.

1. First, lay the cards face-up, in seven rows of three cards – working left to right.
2. Ask your friend to pick a card.

He mustn't tell you which card he has chosen, only whether it is in the first, second or third column.

3. Collect up the cards, in columns this time. Place each card underneath the last. Make sure you collect the column which contains your friend's card second.

4. Next, lay out the cards in seven rows of three cards again.
5. Ask your friend which column his card is in this time, reminding him not to point it out. Collect the cards as you did in step three, collecting the indicated column second.
6. Lay out the cards in seven rows of three again, and for the final time ask your friend to say which column his card is in now.
7. No matter which column he chooses, his card will always be in the middle of that column.

Watch your friend's amazement as you mysteriously pick out his card with a dramatic flourish!

JOKE TIME

Q. What did the water say to the boat?
A. Nothing, it just waved!

DID YOU KNOW?

During World War One, the world's most famous magician and escape artist, Harry Houdini, took a year out from his career to help teach soldiers how to escape from handcuffs.

THE DISAPPEARING COIN

In this trick, you will astonish your audience by making a coin vanish mysteriously before their eyes, using just a glass and a handkerchief (with a little preparation).

You will need: a clear glass / two sheets of plain coloured paper / a pencil / a pair of scissors / sticky tape / a coin / a napkin or a handkerchief.

1. Before your audience arrives, turn the glass upside down on one of the sheets of coloured paper and draw around the rim.
2. Cut out the circle neatly, then use tiny strips of tape to attach it to the top of the glass. When you turn the glass upside down over the other sheet of coloured paper, the circle will blend in.

Place a coin next to the glass on the coloured paper, ready for when your audience comes in.

3. When your audience is ready, tell them that you are about to make the coin disappear right in front of them. Allow them to check that the coin is real then drape the handkerchief over the glass.
4. Place the glass over the coin. Wave your hands and say 'Abracadabra'.
5. Remove the handkerchief to show the coin has disappeared. Ta-da!

THE PEPPER TRICK

For your next trick, you will puzzle and perplex people by magically 'separating' a mixture of water and pepper with just your finger.

You will need: liquid soap or washing-up liquid / a glass of water / a pepper grinder.

1. Before your audience arrives, rub a little soap all over one of your index fingers.
2. When you are ready to perform the trick, place the glass of water in front of you. Tell your audience what you are about to do (this will allow time for the water to stop swirling).
3. Grind a little pepper on to the surface of the water and ask an audience member to separate it from the water with their finger. They will fail. The pepper will stick to their finger.

4. Grind some more pepper over the water. Put your soapy finger in the glass and watch the pepper rush to the edges. The soap simply reduces the water's stretchy surface tension, but your audience will be dazzled.

THE SEVERED THUMB

In this trick, you will shock your audience by presenting them with a 'severed' thumb in a box.

You will need: scissors or a craft knife / a small, rectangular cardboard box with a lid / cotton wool / tomato ketchup.

1. Cut a hole in the bottom of the box, large enough for your thumb to fit through. Arrange some cotton wool around the hole.

2. Push your thumb through the hole and rest it on top of the cotton wool.
3. Now dab some ketchup at the base of your thumb and onto the cotton wool.
4. Put the lid over the box and present it to an unsuspecting friend, explaining that it's a severed thumb.
5. When they lift the lid, wiggle your thumb and watch their stunned reaction!

THE COIN CHALLENGE

In this classic trick you will demonstrate how easy it is to get three coins tails-up, making only three moves, turning over two coins each time. You will then challenge a member of your audience to do the same. They won't be able to do it, but amazingly you will – every time!

You will need: three coins

1. Place the three coins in a row. Coins 1 and 3 must be heads-up and coin 2 must be tails-up.

2. Make three moves, turning over two coins each time like this:
   • Turn over coins 2 and 3.
   • Then turn over coins 1 and 3.
   • Finally, turn over coins 2 and 3 again.
   After your third move, all three coins will be facing tails-up.
3. Now challenge a member of the audience to repeat what you have just done. First you must lay all the coins out facing heads-up – it will make the trick impossible to complete. Magic!

MASTER MIND-READER

This trick will show off your mind-reading skills. You will mysteriously be able to guess an object selected in secret by your audience.

You will need: a selection of red objects in the room / one assistant.

1. Step out of the room while your assistant stays behind. He should ask the audience to choose an object for you to guess when you return. Once this has been done your assistant will call you back into the room.

2. Your assistant should now point at various objects asking you, 'Is this the chosen object?' Magically, you will only say 'Yes' when he points to the item the members of the audience chose.

Your audience might suspect you are using winks or sign language to guess the correct object, but you don't have to. The trick is that you and your assistant have secretly agreed that he will point to a red object immediately before he points to the chosen item. Your audience will be baffled by your psychic abilities and they will beg to know how you did it. Don't tell – a magician never reveals his secrets!

PERFORMANCE TIPS

- Practise your tricks many times before you perform them in front of an audience – that way you'll avoid embarrassing mistakes.
- Make sure that you do all the preparation for the tricks in your show before your audience starts to enter the room.
- Practise adding a confident commentary to accompany your tricks. This will entertain and distract your audience. Add a touch of drama to your voice to give a sense of mystery.
- Never repeat a trick. Your audience might guess how it is done when they see it a second time.

JOKE TIME

Q. What goes up and down while staying still?
A. A staircase!

That's Disgusting

Do you think all animals are cute? Think again. Some can be incredibly gross with foul habits. Here are some facts that will make your hair stand on end.

MONSTER POO

Whale poo can be full of fish eyes and squid beaks that haven't been digested.

EATING POO

Dogs love to eat poo. They'll even eat their own! Some dogs have been known to drag babies' nappies out of the rubbish to eat what they contain.

HUGE AMOUNTS

In zoos, elephants produce massive amounts of poo every day. There's so much of it that many zoos are now looking at ways to use it as an alternative source of fuel.

HINT OF HIPPO

Hippos have a nasty habit of 'poo-flinging'. They wag their tails very fast while pooing. This spreads their unique hippo scent and tells other hippos to stay out of their territory. They also use their poo and wee to attract mates.

POO BUG

Dung beetles get almost all of their food from the dung of other, much larger, animals. They don't actually eat the poo, but instead suck it and squeeze the juice from it.

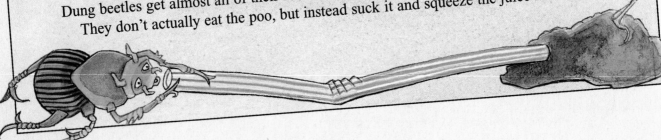

A SECOND TIME AROUND

When cows and sheep have eaten, and their food has gone down, that is not the last time they taste it. After the animals swallow, some of the food is sicked back up into their mouths. They then chew on it again, sometimes for several hours, before swallowing. This is called 'chewing the cud'.

FARTS

Even the tiny termite has a big fart factor. Tests on termite mounds show that, in the right conditions, these little insects could contribute up to one tenth of the natural methane gas in the atmosphere.

NOSE-PICKERS

Many ape species, such as the chimpanzee and orang-utan, pick their noses and eat it.

SPEWING SEABIRD

When threatened, the fulmar gull, whose name means 'foul gull', will hurl its own sick at enemies. Its vomit is very oily and sticks to other birds' feathers, making them difficult to clean – which is a big problem for a seabird.

BELCHING HURTS THE PLANET

Cows and sheep are adding to global warming with their belching. In some countries, scientists add fish oil to their food, to stop them belching so much.

IS THAT CAMEL SPITTING?

Many people believe camels spit. What camels are actually doing is being sick and projecting their stomach contents and saliva in the direction of anyone they feel deserves it.

Yo, Ho, Ho!

Here are some pirate-tastic puzzles for you to play on the high seas. But beware – make a mistake and you'll have to walk the plank! All the answers can be found on page 60.

FLAG MATCH

These pirate flags were flown by famous pirates. Can you spot which one has an exact pair?

a) flown by Blackbeard

b) flown by Calico Jack

c) flown by Black Bart

d) flown by Edmund Condent

e) flown by Captain Dulaien

LIE OR TRUTH?

Here are pirate twin brothers. One always tells the truth and the other always lies. Suggest one question you could ask either twin to work out who is who. It can only be a question with a 'Yes' or 'No' answer.

PIRATE RIDDLES

Here are some pirate riddles to keep your brain as sharp as a cutlass. To give you a clue, they are all things you might find in a pirate's life.

1. I can talk, but I can't understand what I am saying. What am I?

2. I used to be a tree, but now I keep a pirate from falling over.

3. I am all around a pirate, but a pirate does his best to stay out of me.

4. I am something all pirates want and their victims don't want to give up.

AHOY THERE, ME HEARTIES!

This pirate ship and British galleon are having a swashbuckling battle. Can you spot all the things listed below? Take your eye patch off first – if you don't find them all, you'll be swabbing the deck.

1. Can you spot a pirate wearing a red eyepatch?
2. How many parrots can you count?
3. Spot the British sailor holding two swords.
4. Which ship has a major leak in it?
5. Where is the pirate ship's monkey?
6. Where is the wooden-legged pirate?
7. Can you spot two women and a mermaid?
8. Spot a British sailor who's been shot in the leg.

9. Can you spot four pirates swinging between their ship and the galleon on ropes?
10. Can you see a sailor reading a book?
11. Can you spot a pirate who has just leapt out of the way of a cannonball?
12. Spot the pirate leaping overboard with a treasure chest.
13. Can you spot a shark eating a pirate?

BLING UP MY BIKE

If you're bored of your old bike, don't throw it out and beg for a new one. Bling it up! There's a lot of stuff around your house, or things you can buy very cheaply, that will help make your bike the envy of your neighbourhood. Here are some ideas for you to try out.

FUNK UP YOUR FRAME

If you want to make your bike frame look more cool and interesting, this one's for you.

You will need: colourful metal paint / a large and a small paintbrush / newspaper or a dust sheet

1. Choose some metal paint from your local DIY store.
2. Put down lots of newspaper or a large dust sheet in an outdoor area.
3. Load up the large paintbrush with paint and dab it on the frame of your bike (mind the brakes). This will cover the frame with large splodges of paint. Repeat this until it is covered.

4. After the paint has dried, repeat this process of dabbing on paint using the smaller brush. You'll find that the smaller splodges look good against the larger ones. Add more splodges in different colours for a more dramatic effect.
5. Leave to dry before riding your bike.

SOUP UP YOUR SADDLE

Give a plain bike saddle some bling. Why not change it to match the colours of the sports team you support?

You will need: a spare piece of fabric / strong gaffer, duct or electrical tape / scissors.

1. You should be able to get some fabric quite cheaply at a local sewing shop or market. You could also use some old clothes.

2. Cut the fabric so that it's large enough to hang over the edges all around the saddle.

3. Then cut lengths of tape long enough to attach one end of the fabric edge to the other. Do this several times along the underside of the saddle to keep the fabric tight on the top so it doesn't slip.

HOT HANDLEBARS

If you want to give your handlebars an easy facelift, this is all you need to do.

You will need: different colours of wool or string

Simply knot one end of the wool to the handlebars and then keep wrapping it tightly round and round, until you cover them. Then knot the wool at the end. Why not go for a rainbow effect?

WILD AND WACKY WHEELS

A great way to make your spokes and wheels extra-cool is by weaving in some colour.

You will need: different colours of wool or string.

1. Knot one end of wool securely to the top of one spoke, then take it around the next spoke and back again.

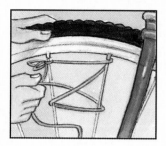

2. Weave the wool in and out between the two spokes in a figure of eight pattern, butting each strand up to the one before.

3. When you get towards the centre of the wheel you will have made a brightly-coloured triangle of wool. Simply knot the wool to the spoke and trim the loose end.

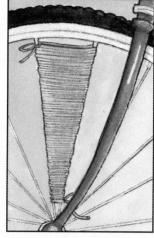
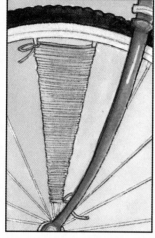

4. Repeat on the opposite side of the wheel, then twice more around other spokes on the wheel to make a star pattern. This will have an amazing effect as the wheels spin around. (Make sure no bits of wool are hanging from your spokes.)

SPOKE CARDS

Bright and colourful cards can liven up your wheels in this quick and easy makeover.

You will need: pieces of card measuring approximately 9 centimetres by 6 centimetres.

Simply weave the cards in and out of a few of the spokes, as shown above. Lots of cards with different colours will look good when the wheels are turning. Why not try using some football or playing cards?

SPOKE STRAWS

Another way to add a bit of cool to your spokes is with some coloured straws.

You will need: scissors / coloured straws.

1. Use the scissors to cut a slit down the length of a number of straws, so that you can open them up.

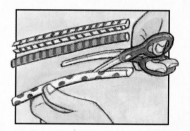

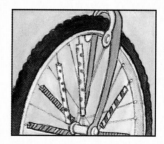

2. Simply slip the straws onto your spokes. The more you fit, the more colourful your spokes will be.

TOP TIP

You will not be very popular if you start painting or taping stuff to a brand new bike. Only bling up an old bike or one from a jumble sale.

JOKE TIME

Q. Why did the turkey pop a wheelie on his bike?
A. To prove he wasn't a chicken!

D.I.Y. FOSSILS

Dinosaurs may be long gone, but there are lots of amazing fossils left behind. Most of what we know about the prehistoric world comes from these fossils, and here's your chance to make your own.

HOW A FOSSIL WAS FORMED

First, a dinosaur had to be 'buried' quickly after it died, so that its body wasn't ripped apart by other dinosaurs, or destroyed by the sun, wind and rain. This might have happened if the dinosaur sank into mud in a riverbed or was buried in a sand storm. Then, over time, the dinosaur was covered up by more earth.

Most of the dinosaur's soft body parts rotted away, leaving just bones and teeth sealed in the earth. Then, over a very long time, the minerals in the earth seeped into the bones, turning them into stone copies of the originals.

HOW TO MAKE YOUR OWN FOSSIL

Follow these easy instructions and you'll soon have an interesting fossil of your own.

You will need: modelling clay or potter's clay / a rolling pin / a small plastic toy / a small brush / petroleum jelly / plaster of Paris / water.

THE MOULD

1. Knead the clay until it is soft. Roll it flat with a rolling pin, until it is about 2 centimetres thick. Make sure your clay is larger on all sides than the toy you're fossilising.

2. Cover the toy with a light layer of petroleum jelly. This will help stop the toy sticking to the clay.

3. Push the toy into the clay.

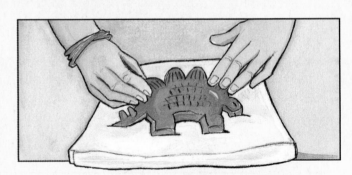

4. Leave it for at least 24 hours, or until it is completely dry, before removing the toy.

THE CAST

1. Prepare the plaster of Paris in a plastic container according to the instructions on the pack. Make enough to fill your mould.
2. Lightly brush the mould with petroleum jelly to keep your cast from sticking.
3. Now pour the plaster of Paris into the mould. The plaster should take 30 minutes to set well enough for you to remove it.
4. Remove the cast and leave it to dry completely.

DID YOU KNOW?

A fossil is a replica, or copy, of the original bone. Scientists make casts to see what the original fossils looked like. Many of the dinosaur skeletons that you see in museums are casts of the originals. This way more people can enjoy amazing dinosaur displays.

MAKE YOUR OWN IMPRINT

Palaeontologists, who study fossils, also find rocks with imprints of plants and shells preserved since prehistoric times. Here's how to make your own.

You will need: a small cup of cold coffee grounds / 200 g plain flour / 175 ml cold water / 6 tsp salt / a baking tray / a sheet of greaseproof paper / a rolling pin / shells and leaves to use for prints.

1. In a large bowl, mix the coffee grounds, flour, water and salt until you have a ball of dough. If the mixture sticks to your fingers add an extra pinch of flour to dry it out a little.
2. Preheat the oven to 150°C / Gas Mark 2 and cover your baking tray with the greaseproof paper.
3. Use your hands to shape the dough into a ball. Then, using a rolling pin, flatten the ball of dough out, by rolling it until it is about 2 centimetres thick.

4. Press leaves and shells into the dough to leave prints (if you are using leaves, press in their underside, where the veins stand out more).

5. Bake your dough in the oven for about an hour and leave to cool on a wire rack. Finally, display your fossil for everyone to admire.

JOKE TIME

Q. What do you call a fossil that doesn't want to work?
A. Lazybones!

UNUSUAL FOSSIL FINDS

Palaeontologists (scientists who study fossils) have found evidence of incredible prehistoric creatures over the years. Here are some real-life stories that have delighted the world.

THE MUMMIFIED DINOSAUR

In 1999, 16-year-old fossil hunter Tyler Lyson was digging for fossils on his uncle's farm in the Hell Creek Formation in North Dakota, USA.
This is an ancient riverbed where 65 million-year-old rocks full of fossils have been found exposed by the wind and rain. The riverbed was also hiding an incredibly rare discovery – the mummified remains of an almost complete dinosaur, with a large amount of tissue and bones still intact and enclosed within its skin.

At first Tyler thought he had just found part of a dinosaur's spine, but as he continued digging, he soon found a small piece of fossilised skin and realised he was on to something special.

A group of palaeontologists soon joined the excavation to help Tyler uncover the rest of the fossil. The dinosaur was a hadrosaur, or 'duck-billed' dinosaur. This was a very special find, as scientists rarely uncover any pieces of skin or tissue, let alone a whole dinosaur.

Because of this discovery scientists have found out some fascinating facts about hadrosaurs. They once thought hadrosaurs were slow movers. By studying its mummified muscles, they now believe that they could run faster than a tyrannosaurus rex at speeds of up to 45 kilometres per hour!

Tyler Lyson went on to work towards a PhD in palaeontology at Yale University in the USA.

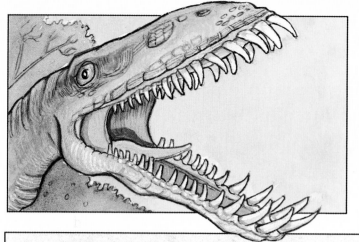

A ROCK AND ROLL FOSSIL

In 2001, Scott Sampson announced the discovery of the fossil of a small, dog-sized dinosaur in Madagascar. The masiakasaurus knopfleri fossil was very unusual – dinosaur teeth are vertical, but this one had several nasty gnashers jutting out from the front of its jaw. Scott and his team named the dinosaur after Mark Knopfler of the rock band called 'Dire Straits,' whose music they were listening to when they made the discovery.

A GIANT TURKEY OF A DINOSAUR

Falcarius utahensis, found in Utah, in the USA, is considered to be one of the most bizarre dinosaurs. These strange creatures were short and dumpy, covered in hair-like feathers, with long, curving claws. They probably looked a bit like giant turkeys!

In 1999 a dealer in illegally dug-up fossils discovered a dinosaur 'graveyard' full of hundreds, if not thousands, of the new species. The man later led palaeontologists to the area so that they could excavate his unusual find.

Scientists found fossils of baby dinosaurs, just hatched from their eggs, as well as young dinosaurs and adults. They believe that the water the dinosaurs drank may have become polluted with bacteria or poisonous gases, which would have wiped out the whole herd at once.

These odd dinosaurs, which lived 125 million years ago, provide an important link between older, meat-loving dinos and later plant-chompers.

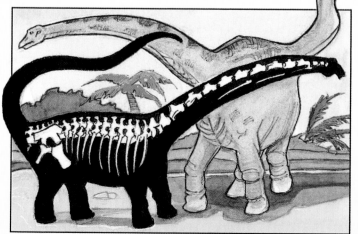

THE BIGGEST DINOSAUR EVER

In 2000, the fossil of a futalognkosaurus, one of the largest dinosaurs to ever roam the earth, was discovered in Patagonia, in Argentina. It would have measured 32 metres from its head to its tail and stood a massive four storeys high.

Amazingly, 80 per cent of the fossil was complete. This find is remarkable, considering that other giant dinosaur skeletons found so far are usually only around 10 per cent complete.

SURVIVAL

SELF-PRESERVATION

BY JENNY SIKLOS
Boys' Annual Writer

Here are two amazing true stories, that show you never know when you may get into a difficult situation and have to use all your wits to survive.

IN 2003, 28-YEAR-OLD Aron Ralston from Aspen, Colorado, USA, was hiking in a national park in Utah. He was an experienced hiker who had walked most of Colorado's highest peaks.

As he was passing through a narrow canyon, a boulder fell on him, pinning his right arm down. The boulder weighed around 400 kilos and couldn't be moved.

For five days, Aron lay with the boulder crushing his arm. He tried moving the rock with some of his equipment, but it wouldn't budge. Then he began chipping away at the boulder. After ten exhausting hours and just a little pile of rock dust to show for it, he gave up.

Aron began to despair and thought he was certainly going to die. So, he filmed a video 'goodbye' to his parents and etched his name, birth date and that day's date, with RIP above it, into the canyon wall.

Next morning, Aron had a vision of a three-year-old boy being scooped up by a one-armed man. He knew he was seeing himself in the future with his son and decided he had to do something drastic.

Aron Ralston, 28, knew time was running out.

Pulling out his penknife, Aron began the process of cutting off his arm from below the elbow. He knew that his penknife was not strong enough to cut through the bone. So he broke the bones against the rock himself. Then, all his knife had to go through would be tissue, muscle and veins.

He tied some cloth tightly around his arm to slow down the bleeding and cut until he was free. Although he was in terrible pain, Aron slowly made his way down to the bottom of the canyon and started looking for help.

Luckily, he came across a Dutch family. The Dutch man stayed with Aron, while his wife and son went to get help and were spotted by a rescue helicopter.

Aron survived and wrote a book about his experiences.

ISLAND SURVIVORS

BY A STAFF WRITER

IN 2004 AN 11-YEAR-OLD Australian boy, Stephen Nona, and his younger brother, two sisters and their parents were making a dinghy trip to Thursday Island in the Torres Strait – a body of water which lies between Australia and New Guinea.

During the trip, the engine stopped. As Stephen's father tried to fix it, the boat capsized, tossing them all overboard.

Stephen's parents urged him and his sisters to try and swim to an outcrop of rocks that was visible from the boat. The parents stayed with the boat, holding their youngest son up on a lifejacket. As the children began to swim, Stephen looked back to see his parents gesturing at him to keep going – it was the last time he saw them or his brother.

Mr and Mrs Nona urged their children to swim to safety.

The three children reached the rocks and scanned the sea for mother, father and brother, but realised all three were gone. As night fell the children huddled together for warmth.

The next day, they searched the shore and found oysters on the rocks to eat.

By the fourth day, Stephen realised that they could not survive by staying where they were. He told his sisters that they'd have to swim. Stephen was a strong swimmer, but his sisters were not and didn't like the idea. However, they knew that they had no other choice.

The children managed to swim a total of 6 kilometres to the island of Matu, where they found coconuts. Their first proper drink in four days was of coconut milk.

The children kept watch for rescuers.

Three days later, they spotted their uncle's search boat. They ran towards him, crying and yelling, desperately frightened that he wouldn't spot them. Thankfully, he did and they were taken immediately to hospital.

Their ordeal was over. They had suffered dehydration (too little water), sunburn and shock. And now they had to survive the reality of having lost their parents and younger brother.

In 2005 the Australian government awarded each of the children medals for their incredible bravery.

The children received medals for bravery.

BRING THE FUN BACK

Need to get off the sofa and have some fun? Want to find some things to keep your family and friends entertained? Here are some great ways to make them laugh.

THE FUNNY QUESTION GAME

Players must guess what famous person, creature or thing you are, by asking questions that have a 'yes' or 'no' answer. This game works best with a large group of people.

You will need: a pen / some small pieces of paper, one per player / some sticky tape.

1. Write the name of a famous person, creature, or thing on each piece of paper.

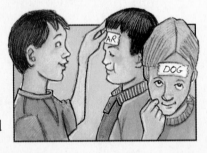

2. Tape a piece of paper to each player's forehead, or to their back, so they can't read it themselves.

3. Players must take turns to ask a question to help them guess what is written on their label. Sample questions might be, 'Do I smell?' or 'Do I suck blood?' or 'Do I live in a swamp?'

4. Keep playing until everyone has guessed what their label says.

YOU'RE SUCH A POSER

In this game, you must try to get the 'poser' to strike a specific pose using cheers and boos.

1. The 'poser' goes out of the room while the other players agree on the pose he will have to strike. For example, it could be sitting with arms and legs crossed or standing on one foot, etc.

2. Tell the 'poser' to come back and to start striking different poses. Everyone else must now cheer when he is getting close to the correct position, or boo and hiss when he is completely off. They musn't give any directions.

3. As soon as the poser strikes the correct pose, everyone gives him a round of applause.

JOKE TIME

Q. What do you call an elephant in a telephone box?
A. Stuck!

ROCK, PAPER, SCISSORS

Two players call out, 'rock, paper, scissors', while pounding their fists up and down in the air three times. On 'scissors', each player must choose which of three actions they will show with their hand: a fist for rock, a flat hand for paper, or two fingers for scissors.

To determine the winner, check the following:

- Rock beats scissors because rock blunts scissors.
- Scissors beat paper because they cut up paper.
- Paper beats rock because it can wrap up a rock.

BALLOON RACE

Players get into pairs, then each pair takes a partly-inflated balloon and puts it between their heads. They must then race down a course to a finish line without using their hands and without letting the balloon drop. The first two over the finish line without dropping their balloon are the winners.

WHO AM I?

All players must go out of the room and secretly draw a picture of themselves that 'sums them up'. All the pictures are then displayed and everyone has to guess who drew each one. The drawer then explains what they have drawn and why they chose to draw that image. Make sure your friends and family know they will have to explain their drawings, otherwise they will just try to be funny.

QUICK GAMES

WHO DID THAT?

Ask your friends and family to write a small description of something amazing or unusual that they have done on a piece of paper and put them all into a hat. Then, one by one, take each piece of paper out and read it. Everyone then tries to guess who did what. This game is sure to surprise.

'TRUE OR FALSE' VERSION ONE

Ask each person to tell a story about something they've experienced, for example their most embarrassing moment, or the best day of their life so far. When they are finished the rest of the players must decide if the story is true or false.

'TRUE OR FALSE' VERSION TWO

Get your friends to sit in a circle and take it in turns describing three different things about themselves. Two of the things should be true and one of them should be false. Before the game begins, give everyone a pen and paper, so they can have a think and write down their three ideas.

Sample sentences could be: 'I have been to 20 different countries. I won't eat anything that lives underwater. I once saw the Queen.'

Then, everyone should vote on which of the three things is false.

THE MEMORY TRAY

Find 15 interesting objects, place them on a tray and cover it with a cloth. When everyone is ready, remove the cloth and ask them to study the tray's contents for 30 seconds. Then cover the tray again. Now ask each person to write down all the items that they can remember. The one who remembers the most items correctly wins.

STARING CONTEST

Why not have an old-fashioned staring competition? Stare at your friend and see who can resist blinking, or laughing, longest.

ARM WRESTLING

An arm-wrestling contest will reveal who is the strongest member of your family.

PHOTO FUN

Have a camera handy to take plenty of shots of you and your friends and family playing these games. You can laugh at them later!

MAKE SOME GOO

Are you a fan of all things gross and slimy? If you are, then you're going to love making goo.

You will need: water / a jug / 3 tbsp of borax, also known as sodium borate, available from some chemists and hardware stores / 5 tbsp of water / 5 tbsp of PVA glue / a mixing bowl / green food colouring / a large zip-lock plastic bag.

1. Pour 300 millilitres of cold water in to a jug and carefully add 3 tablespoons of borax. Stir well and put to one side.
2. Now add 5 tablespoons of cold water to 5 tablespoons of PVA glue in a mixing bowl. Stir them together until smooth. Then add the food colouring (just a few drops) and stir again.
3. Now pour about 1 teaspoon of the borax mixture into the bowl and stir. You should immediately notice the slime effect. Slowly add the rest of the borax mixture, stirring all the time until it's all in.
4. As you mix, the slime will form. As soon as all the borax is added you should be able to squash your goo between your hands like dough.

Keep your goo in the zip-lock bag, preferably in the fridge. That'll keep it gooey for much longer.

QUALITY TIME WITH YOUR SLIME

One of the joys of your new slime is the disgusting noises it makes. Put yours in a clean jar. Now ask your friends to stick a finger in and pull it out quickly. Where have you heard that sound before?

HALLOWEEN FUN

To turn the gross factor up, add rubbery worms, flies and spiders to your slime. Try adding different food colours for new effects. This makes a really disgusting decoration for a Halloween party.

• TOP TIPS FOR SAFE GOO-ING •

• Be careful not to let young children eat the borax – it can be harmful.
• Remember, always wash your hands after handling goo.
• Don't put goo in anybody's hair – it won't come out, even in the bath.

A BOY PHARAOH AND HIS MUMMY

The boy king, Tutankhamun, is the most famous pharaoh in history.
His incredible burial chamber and treasure continue to fascinate the world today.

Tutankhamun was an Egyptian king (known as a pharaoh). He ruled Egypt in the 14th century BC. He was only about 19 when he died. Some scientists believe that he broke his leg a few days before he died. They think the leg became badly infected causing his death. Like all royalty, Tutankhamun couldn't just be buried, he had to be mummified – a process that took 70 days.
Here's how to mummify someone.

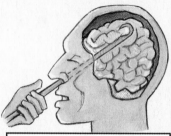

2. Remove the fluids and vital organs (lungs, liver, etc.), but leave the heart in place.

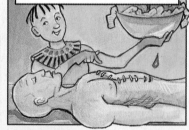

1. Remove the brain with a long hook and pull out bits at a time, through the nostrils.

3. Treat the body with wine, spices and finally natron (a kind of salt), to dry it out.

4. Fill in any sunken bits with linen.

5. Add false eyes to create a more life-like look.

6. Wrap the body in 13 layers of linen that have been soaked in oils.
7. Place amulets and charms within the linen, to keep away evil spirits.

8. Place a solid gold death mask over the mummy's face.

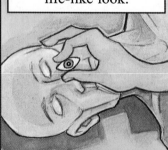

9. Place the body and mask inside a solid gold coffin, then inside three more coffins.

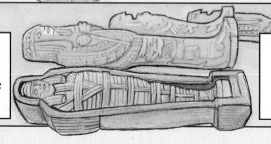

10. Put the vital organs in jars, ready for the burial chamber.
You are done!

THE GREAT PYRAMID MAZE

Tutankhamun was buried with a huge amount of amazing treasure in a chamber in an area called the Valley of the Kings. The location of the chamber was kept secret to prevent people stealing the treasure from the tomb.

Most pharaohs were buried inside pyramids, and the people who designed pyramids had to create lots of ways to try and keep out grave robbers. They blocked passages with massive stones or made some lead nowhere. They installed trapdoors, and made sure the pyramid had no obvious entry point. But grave robbers still managed to get in and steal the treasures.

Even the mummified bodies weren't safe. During the Middle Ages, mummies were regularly stolen and ground into powders – people believed they held magical powers. Sometimes mummies' bandages were used to make paper and their bodies burned for fuel.

Now it's your chance to pretend you're an Egyptian grave robber. See if you can find your way to the chamber full of treasure. The answer can be found on page 60.

It is widely believed that the Great Pyramid at Giza is about 4,600 years old.

The Great Pyramid is over 140 metres high.

The corridors of pyramids are extremely narrow.

Each block of a pyramid is thought to weigh about 2 tonnes.

Archaeologists now believe that the Great Pyramid was built from the inside out.

START

The staircases can be extremely steep and treacherous.

IT'S ALL EGYPTIAN TO ME

From gods to hieroglyphs, these pages will take you further into the incredible, mystic world of the Ancient Egyptians. All answers can be found on page 60.

The Ancient Egyptians believed in many gods. Each one controlled a different part of peoples' lives in this world and in the 'after life'. Look at these pictures of Egyptian gods and see if you can match them to their names and descriptions.

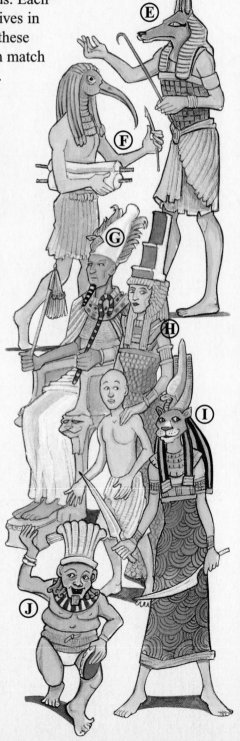

1. OSIRIS
God of the dead, ruler of the underworld.

2. RA
The sun god and most important of all the gods.

3. HORUS
The falcon-headed god and protector of the pharaoh.

4. SOBEK
The crocodile-headed god who controlled water supplies.

5. THOTH
The ibis-headed god of writing and knowledge.

6. HATHOR
The cow-horned god of love and joy.

7. SEKHMET
The lioness god of war.

8. BES
The dwarf god of happiness.

9. ISIS
The wife of Osiris, who took care of children and women.

10. ANUBIS
The jackal-headed god of mummification and the dead.

MAKE YOUR OWN EGYPTIAN SCARAB

A scarab is a large beetle and was regarded as sacred by the Ancient Egyptians. Scarabs lay their eggs in animal dung – but the Egyptians didn't know this. When they saw beetles emerge from balls of dung they thought it was magic. The Egyptians made ornaments in the shape of scarabs to ward off evil spirits.

Why not make your own magical scarab by following these easy steps?

You will need: self-hardening clay / a small paper clip / a toothpick / paint

1. Roll the clay into an oval-shaped ball, about 5 centimetres long.
2. Push a paper clip deep into the top of the clay, so that only a small loop sticks out.

3. Now put the clay on a flat surface and press down slightly to flatten the top.
4. With a toothpick, press dents in the clay to indicate the head, eyes and wings.

5. Allow the clay to dry and then paint it.
6. Hang your scarab by your bedroom door to ward off your friends and family!

HIEROGLYPHS

Hieroglyphs were the Ancient Egyptian form of writing. Symbols were used to stand for a letter or a whole word. The list of hieroglyphs is long and complex. Here is a selection:

Using the list of hieroglyphs, try to write a message to one of your friends.

Now see if you can work out the sentence below. (The Egyptians didn't have a sign for the letter E, so all the Es have been added already.)

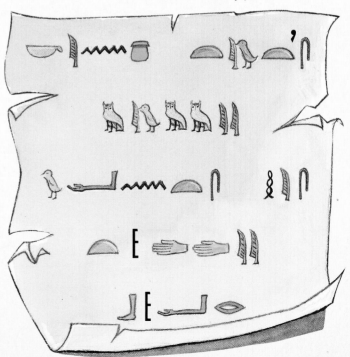

CARTOONING CRAZINESS

Cartoons are a cool way to show your creative side. With these top tips and foolproof instructions you'll be making your very own crazy characters in no time.

BODY BASICS

When you draw a figure, you must pay attention to the way you want your character to stand or move – the position of each part of the body is very important to make it look natural and realistic.

When you first start cartooning the 'bean' body is a great basic type of body to work from. Use a pencil to draw your figure as this will allow you to rub out certain areas.

1. Start with an 'action line'. This is a line that runs through the body and head, like a big spine, and helps decide the position of the body.

2. Next, draw the head as a round or oblong bean.

3. Now draw the bean body.

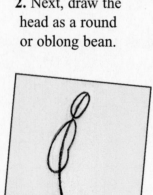

4. Next add your figure's legs and feet.

5. Add arms and hands, as well as all the details of the face and clothing to finish your bean figure.

Here are some examples of bean-figure poses and actions for you to try. Trace over them to help you get more comfortable with the movement of your pencil when cartooning.

DID YOU KNOW?

The first attempts at cartooning started tens of thousands of years ago. Cave paintings have been found showing animals with multiple legs which make them look as if they are moving.

FIRST FACES

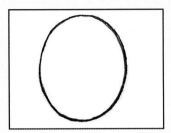

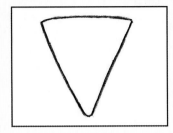

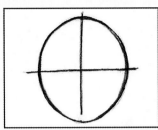

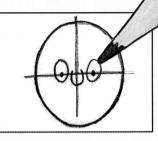

1. To draw a face, start with the basic shape of a character's head – it could be round, oblong, square…

… or even a triangle.

2. Draw a cross through the middle of the shape, as shown. This will help you position the features and hair properly.

3. Now position the eyes and nose on the horizontal line (the line that runs across the page) as shown here.

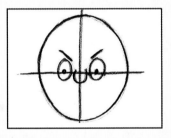

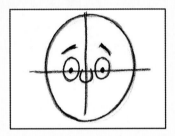

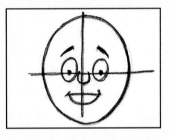

4. Give the eyes some expression by adding eyebrows – pointing down for angry…

… or have them arched upwards to show surprise.

5. Then position the mouth at the centre of the vertical (up and down) line.

6. Finally, add some hair and ears.

EXPRESSIONS

The key to drawing a good face is to exaggerate its emotions or make it look 'larger than life'. Here are some examples:

sad

laughing

shocked

scared

puzzled

crying

happy

~ 33 ~

• YOUR •
AMAZING ROOM

Your room probably has four walls, a window or two and a bed. Boring! But it doesn't need to be. Here are some fun projects to help make your room look really cool.

MEMORY BOARD

Make a memory board for all the stuff you collect.

You will need: a large corkboard with hooks on the back / a piece of fabric, larger than the corkboard / scissors / a stapler – a staple gun will make it easier / ribbon (why not use ribbon in the colours of the team you support?) / drawing pins.

1. Lay the fabric out on a table or on the floor and place the corkboard on top of it. Carefully trim the fabric so that it is at least 4 centimetres larger than the corkboard all the way around.

2. Staple the edges of the fabric to the back of the frame. Pull it tight across the front to avoid wrinkles.

3. Measure several strips of ribbon to run diagonally across the board from one corner to the other. Make sure each one is long enough to be stapled to the back of the frame. Space them out evenly.

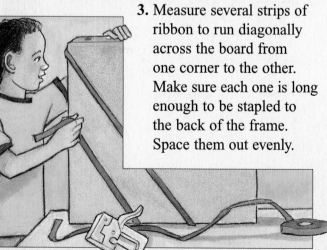

4. Now do the same in the opposite direction, so that you end up with diamond shapes on the front of the board.

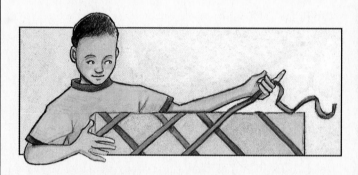

5. Turn the board over and staple the end of each ribbon, keeping them spaced evenly. Remember to pull the ribbon tight when you staple it down.

6. Push in a drawing pin to hold the ribbon flat at each point where it crosses.

7. Now just hang up your memory board and tuck your favourite pictures and mementos under the ribbons.

LIGHT SWITCH FRAME

Make the dullest item in your room – the light switch – into something exciting and fun with a little imagination and creativity.

You will need: a pencil / tracing paper / a sheet of coloured card / scissors / paints or stickers / some sticky tack.

1. Trace the shape of the light switch panel with a pencil onto the tracing paper. Then cut out the shape of the panel to make a template and lay it over the card.

2. Now draw around the tracing paper template and cut out the centre, leaving a space in the middle of the card for the light switch.

3. Cut the outer edges of the frame in zig-zags, or wavy lines, to make them more interesting.
4. Decorate with paint and stickers and then allow your frame to dry.
5. Position the frame over your light switch and attach it to the wall with some sticky tack.

BLACKBOARD WALL

Plain bedroom walls are so boring. Why not ask your parents if you can have a blackboard wall that you can write and doodle on instead?

First, buy a tin of blackboard paint. Then decide how large you want the 'blackboard' area on your wall to be.

Prepare the wall according to the tin's instructions. If you've got a little brother or sister, make sure they will be able to reach, so that they can have fun on the blackboard, too.

When the paint has dried, you will be able to leave notes for your friends and family. You could leave yourself messages about what you are up to each evening, or practise your artistic skills with blackboard chalks.

JOKE TIME

Q. Why did the boy bring toilet paper to the birthday party?
A. Because he was a party pooper!

PUZZLES AND PARASITES

Parasites must be among the grossest creatures around. A parasite lives off, or inside, another creature's body – which gives them a high yuck factor. Learn a little bit about them by trying your hand at these puzzles. All the answers can be found on pages 60 and 61.

TRUE OR FALSE

How much do you know about parasites already? See if you know whether the following facts are true or false.

1. Tapeworms come out of a creature's mouth when they are ready to leave its body.

2. Scoleciphobia is the name given to a fear of being infested with parasitic worms.

3. Maggots were used by military doctors during World War Two to treat wounded soldiers.

4. The pork tapeworm can live in a human's brain.

5. The bubonic plague, a disease largely spread by fleas, is ancient history and we don't have to worry about it anymore.

6. Head lice jump from one child to another.

7. Nits start biting from the moment they hatch.

8. Parasites are only found in tropical countries.

THE LIFE CYCLE OF HEAD LICE

Head lice are parasites that love to live off human blood. If you get them they can make you itch like mad. Like most parasites, head lice go through a series of big changes in their lives. See if you can put the changes in the correct order.

A. After 2 days the larva goes through its first moult – shedding its skin – a major physical change.

B. The louse is now an adult and finds a mate.

C. Just 33 days after hatching, the louse dies.

D. Then it goes through another moult and then another.

E. Just one or two days later the female louse lays her first eggs.

F. The female louse finds a shaft of hair to lay her eggs on.

G. The head louse larva (baby) hatches and enters the world.

H. She keeps on laying four to eight eggs per day for another 16 days.

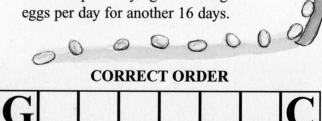

CORRECT ORDER

G					C

DID YOU KNOW?

It is widely believed that the longest tapeworm ever found was in 1991 inside Sally Mae Wallace of Mississippi, USA. Some say doctors removed the worm from her mouth, but it may have come out of her bottom! It measured an astonishing 11 metres in length.

FLEAS

These parasites love to suck blood and make people and animals itch. They start their lives as small worm-like larvae and then spin themselves a cocoon. After they emerge from the cocoon, they look for some hair or fur to live in.

How many fleas can you find on this close up of a boy's scalp?

CANINE KILLER

The heartworm is a small, thread-like worm that can kill a dog by infecting its heart and lungs. In the USA, dogs are given a monthly pill to help them avoid getting this parasite.
Rover the dog needs to take his monthly pill. Which path will take him to it?

A
B
C
D

JOKE TIME

Q. How can you tell which end of a worm is which?
A. Tickle in the middle and see which end laughs!

MEXICAN FIESTA

No one throws a party quite like the people of Mexico. So, why not follow the ideas on these pages and hold a Mexican fiesta for your friends?

FIESTA PIÑATA

A piñata is a large Mexican party decoration, filled with sweets or little presents and great fun to make. It must be smashed open with a stick before the sweets can be eaten.

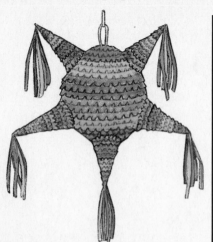

You will need: 1 large balloon / 1 piece of thick string, at least 60 cm long / newspaper / a paintbrush / 250 ml water and 250 ml PVA glue, mixed together / a pin / scissors / 5 sheets of A4 card / undiluted PVA glue or sticky tape / paper clips / lots of colourful tissue paper or poster paint.

HOW TO MAKE A STAR PIÑATA

1. Blow up your balloon and tie the neck into a knot. Then tie the string tightly around the neck and rest the balloon in a dish to hold it steady.
2. Now tear the newspaper into long strips. Brush each strip with the glue/water mixture, and lay them across the balloon – the pieces should overlap one another. Make sure that all of the balloon is covered, but leave the string poking out. You will need to cover the balloon with five layers of paper to make it strong enough. Wait for each layer to dry before adding another one.

3. When the fifth layer has dried, cover the whole thing with glue mixture and leave overnight.

4. The next day, pop the balloon with a pin. Pull the string to one side and cut a small flap near the top and remove the balloon. Fill the piñata with sweets (there are recipes for some tasty treats you could try on page 40). Glue the flap down again securely.

5. The next step is to make the star's points. Roll each piece of A4 card into a cone shape and stick the edges together with undiluted PVA glue. Secure the edges with paper clips while the glue sets then cut off the triangular corners at the base of each cone.

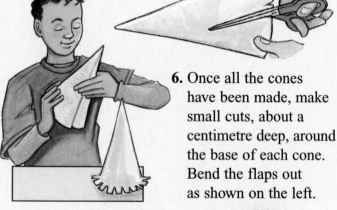

6. Once all the cones have been made, make small cuts, about a centimetre deep, around the base of each cone. Bend the flaps out as shown on the left.

7. Take each cone and paint glue onto the underside of the flaps, then press down onto your piñata. They will need to be held down for a while to ensure that they stick properly. Space the rest of the cones evenly around the balloon, then leave to dry.

DECORATING YOUR PIÑATA

You can just choose your piñata's colours and decorate it with poster paints, but for a more authentic-looking alternative, follow these instructions.

1. Cut the sheets of tissue paper into strips about 2.5 x 8 centimetres. At the edge of every strip cut notches 1 centimetre deep as you did on the base of the cones.

2. Now start gluing the uncut edge of the strips to the piñata, so that the notches stick out.

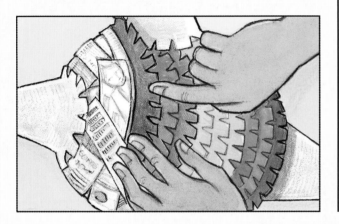

Overlap the strips, placing one layer over the next, so that the notches show in each row. The traditional piñata design is to add rows of coloured stripes – a few rows of red then a few rows of yellow and so on, but you can arrange your colours any way you like.

3. Cover the cones in the same way.

4. Next, cut 30 to 40 strips of tissue paper, at least 30 centimetres long. Glue several to the ends of each of the cones to create long tassels for a truly traditional Mexican look.

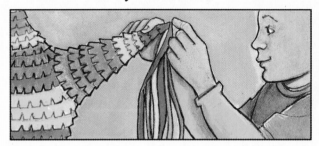

Ahora, puedes tener diversión con tu piñata! (*A-or-a pwe-thays ten-air dee-ver-see-on con too pee-nya-ta*). Now you can have fun with your piñata!

HOW TO BREAK YOUR PIÑATA

Now it is time to break open your piñata.

It is best to hang it from a strong washing line or a tree branch. Hang it in a way that allows you to raise or lower it while someone is hitting it – this will add to the excitement of the game.

Each person takes a turn to be blindfolded and is given the stick to hit the piñata. The stick can be anything from a broomstick to a baseball bat. Everyone gets three goes, with the youngest going first each time.

Be sure to keep everyone well back as each person has a go, so no one gets bashed with the stick. Remember, the key is to break the piñata open, so that the sweets come out. If you knock a bit off, you don't get another chance and the next person has a go at smashing it open.

The game ends when the sweets start tumbling out.

PINTO BEAN FUDGE

Here's a tasty recipe that actually contains something good for you – beans! Wait for your friends to taste just how delicious it is before you surprise them with the mystery ingredient.

You will need: 1 tin of pinto beans, drained and cooked / 60 ml milk / 1 tbsp vanilla essence / 170 g dark chocolate / 100 g unsalted butter / 500 g icing sugar / 20 cm square baking tin / greaseproof paper.

1. Cook the beans as directed on the tin. Place them in a large bowl, pour in the milk and mash them together with a potato masher or fork. Stir in the vanilla and set aside.

2. In a small saucepan, melt the chocolate and butter together over a low heat. Be careful not to let it burn.

3. Stir the melted chocolate and butter into the bean mixture, then gradually mix in the icing sugar. Towards the end you may need to squash the mixture with your hands to blend it thoroughly.

4. Lightly butter the baking tin and line with greaseproof paper, then spread the mix over the base. Chill in the refrigerator for at least one hour, or until set.

5. Once set, cut the fudge into squares and wrap them up in pieces of greaseproof paper.

CHOCOLATE PECAN FUDGE

These are extremely easy to make and are yummy!

You will need: 450 g dark chocolate / 75 g unsalted butter / 400 g tin sweetened condensed milk / ½ tsp vanilla essence / 150 g pecan nuts / 20 cm square baking tin / greaseproof paper.

1. In a small saucepan, melt the chocolate, butter and condensed milk together over a low heat. Be careful not to let it burn.

2. Once they are completely blended, take the pan off the heat and stir in the vanilla essence.

3. Put aside 16 pecan nuts for the topping, then roughly chop the remaining nuts and stir them into the chocolaty mix.

4. Lightly butter the baking tin and line with greaseproof paper then pour in the mixture. Top with whole pecans.

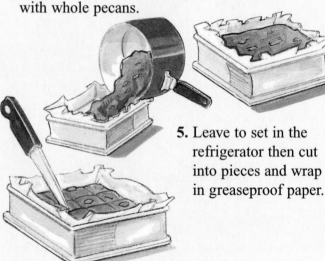

5. Leave to set in the refrigerator then cut into pieces and wrap in greaseproof paper.

When your fudge is wrapped and ready, fill up your piñata. Now all you have to do is decorate your house and get ready for the fiesta.

• WARNING •

**Whenever you are heating things in the kitchen make
sure there is an adult around to help you.**

DID YOU KNOW?

Mexicans celebrate the Day of the Dead or El día de los muertos (*El dee-ah they los mwer-tos*) on 1st November every year. It's a day to remember, celebrate, and for some people, try and communicate with dead friends and relatives. Many families visit graveyards and have lively picnics on their loved ones' graves.

PAPEL PICADO

Here's a traditional Mexican decoration to help make your fiesta complete.

You will need: scissors / colourful tissue paper / a long string for hanging the flags on / sticky tape

1. Cut the tissue paper into A4-sized sheets.
2. Fold the sheets in half, then in half again, and half again.

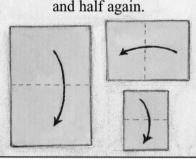

3. Cut small shapes into the paper around the edges. Try experimenting with the shapes – can you make a skull?

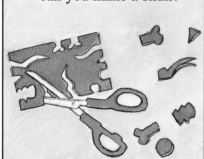

4. When you are finished, carefully unfold to see the fun flag you have created.

5. Your string needs to be long enough to go from one corner of your party room to the other. Lay the string on a table and tape a flag to it lengthways. Then, leaving a small space, attach the next flag, and then the next, until the string is filled. Now you're ready to hang it up. Of course, you can do shorter strings to go over windows and doorways, too.

HANDY SPANISH PHRASES

Buenos días (*Bwey-nos dee-ahs*) – Good morning
¡Hola! (*Oh-la*) – Hi!
Me llamo… (*May yah-mo…*) – My name is…
Adiós (*Ah-the-os*) – Goodbye
Soy de inglaterra (*Soy they ing-la-tear-a*) – I'm from England
No hablo español (*No ah-blow es-pan-yol*) – I don't speak Spanish.

SHARK ATTACK!

Swimming in the sea is great fun – or is it? The trouble with the sea is sometimes you can't see what's lurking beneath the waves. Here are some facts about the undisputed kings of the sea – sharks.

There are three main types of shark attack:

1. THE 'HIT AND RUN' ATTACK

In the surf zone, a shark's target is not swimmers or surfers. Scientists think sharks sometimes confuse bony humans with tasty seals. It could also be a 'dominance' display by the shark wanting the human to get out of its territory.

2. THE 'BUMP AND BITE' ATTACK

These attacks usually happen in deep water to divers or swimmers. The shark first circles and then bumps its victim before it bites. In this kind of attack, the shark usually bites a few times and the victim often dies.

3. THE 'SNEAK' ATTACK

This is an attack that comes out of nowhere. As with the 'bump and bite' attack, the victim often suffers fatal injuries.

CANNIBALS OF THE SEA

In the confusion of a feeding frenzy, when many sharks are trying to eat at once, the ravenous creatures will bite and eat anything in their path. If a shark is injured it may even get attacked by other sharks.

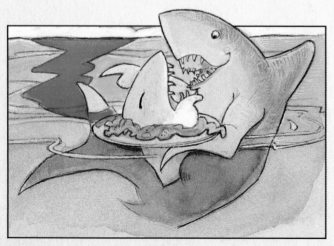

THE TOP SHARK OFFENDERS

There are over 350 species of shark in the world, but only three make up the majority of the serious or deadly attacks on humans. These are:
• the great white shark (carcharodon carcharias)
• the tiger shark (galeocerdo cuvier)
• the bull shark (carcharhinus leucas).

BOOGIE-BOARDING GOES WRONG

In California, in 1998, 16-year-old Jonathan Kathrein was boogie-boarding in the ocean when his hand brushed against something that felt a lot like sandpaper. He began to head for shore, but what turned out to be a 3.5 metre shark clamped its teeth around his right leg. Jonathan tried desperately to free himself and eventually grabbed the shark's gills – at which point, fortunately, the shark let him go. Jonathan then had a terrifying swim to the shore, hoping the shark wouldn't follow.

After seven hours of surgery, the doctors managed to save Jonathan's leg. Eventually, he made a full recovery and still surfs today.

After the attack, many people offered their boats to Jonathan so he could go out to sea, hunt the shark down and kill it, but Jonathan felt this was wrong. 'It wasn't the shark's fault,' he said.

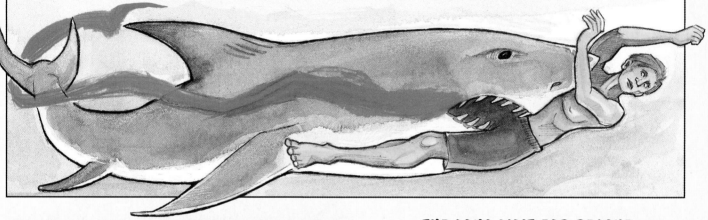

THE LONG WAIT FOR RESCUE

During World War Two, a US Navy cruiser, the USS Indianapolis, was sunk by a Japanese submarine in the middle of the night in the Philippine Sea.

It was estimated that between 800 and 900 men survived the sinking by escaping into the water.

The survivors spent all night huddled in groups trying to stay afloat in the sea, but the morning brought an even more terrifying threat. Tiger sharks were spotted 'sniffing' around the men. Survivors reported that some were 9 metres in length.

The sharks began to attack the men on the edges of the groups. Then they would stop for a few hours, only to come back later to start feeding all over again.

Over 300 men were eaten alive in the five days before rescuers arrived. Even as men were being pulled from the water, the sharks kept ripping at their bodies.

It is the worst recorded shark attack in history.

JOKE TIME

Q. What's a shark's favourite game?
A. Swallow the leader!

TOP TIPS FOR AVOIDING A SHARK ATTACK

• Never swim, dive or surf alone.
• Don't swim near sandbars, steep drop-offs
or channels – these are spots that sharks love to feed in.
• Don't swim in dirty water where the visibility is low.
• Never swim if you have a nosebleed –
sharks can smell blood up to 0.4 kilometres away.
• Don't wear any jewellery that shines. Sharks will
think it's the scales of a tasty fish. You
should also avoid wearing brightly-coloured clothes.
• Never swim at dusk or at night – this is prime
shark-feeding time.
• Don't splash around a lot. This attracts sharks,
as they think you're a struggling fish or seal.
• Don't swim near fishermen as sharks are attracted
to the fish and bloody bait in the water.

THE SHARK IS THE REAL VICTIM

Despite these stories, sharks definitely don't deserve their
bad reputation. Your chances of being killed by a bee sting,
a snake bite or by lightning are far greater than being killed by a shark.

The shark is a marvellous creature and vitally important to the
ecosystem of the oceans. Some experts claim that over 100 million
sharks are killed by fishing and hunting each year. Compare that to
the fewer than 100 people killed in shark attacks in recent years.
It's pretty easy to see who's coming off worst!

Sharks are being caught and killed at a far faster rate than
they can reproduce. Some shark conservation groups expect that at
least 20 species of shark will be extinct by the year 2017.

DID YOU KNOW?

• Sharks are lightning fast. The blue shark can reach
speeds of nearly 70 kilometres per hour in short bursts.
• Sharks have been around for 400 million years –
200 million years before the earliest known dinosaur.
• Some of the bizarre objects found inside a shark's stomach
include a man in a full suit of armour and a torpedo.

INDOOR GOLF

Who needs the local golf course when your home can provide a perfect putt? The aim is to get the ball into a saucepan or frying pan, but first, you'll have to hit tricky targets and get round lots of hazards on the way.

BUILDING YOUR COURSE

Building a golf course in your own house can be great fun. Work out ahead of time which rooms can be included in your course. It might be better to keep away from some – such as the one with the expensive widescreen TV!

You will need: a traditional umbrella, walking or broomstick that can be used as a golf club (or you could always use a real golf club) / as many saucepans or frying pans as you can get / some 'hazards', which could include boxes, empty cardboard tubes, CDs, DVDs, toys, aluminium foil, shoeboxes / sticky tape / masking tape / a small rubber ball – a golf ball is too hard and could damage the furniture.

TARGETS

To make the course more challenging, mark 'targets', such as a spot on a skirting board, with masking tape. Part of a 'fairway' can involve getting through or around hazards and hitting the target, before ending up at the hole itself.

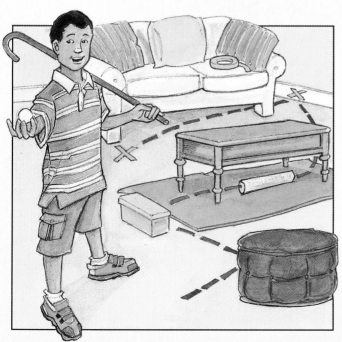

READY-MADE FAIRWAY

You won't have to create every fairway. Your stairs are perfect and extremely challenging. Put a saucepan 'hole' at the bottom to sink the ball into. You can also use beds, dining and coffee tables, etc.

PUTT PERFECT

This is miniature golf, so there are no hard 'drives'. A drive is the hard hit that a golfer does at the beginning of a hole. Instead, you will be 'putting' your way around.

A putt is the slow, careful tapping action that a golfer uses when the ball is close to the hole. The key to putting is keeping your swing light and soft. Focus on the ball and where it is in relation to the hole. Never raise your club over your head.

Careful putting will help you avoid obstacles and keep your shots more accurate.

CREATING HAZARDS

Here are some ideas for holes that you could try to create:

'BOUNCE OFF THE BOXES'

Collect five shoeboxes or cereal boxes. Pop something inside to weigh them down. Line them up in a wide zigzag pattern. You must hit the side of each box, in order, before going on to the hole.

THE 'TUBE'

Cut the cardboard tube from inside a roll of kitchen towel in half, lengthways. Tape the ends of the roll down to the floor. Now, see if you can putt through it to get to the next hazard.

THE 'SWISH'

This hazard requires the help of a friend. Ask him to stand in front of the marked hole. He should hold something like a broom or another golf club. As you try to make your putt, he should slowly swish his 'stick' back and forth near to the ground, hoping to knock your ball away from the hole. You will have to play your next shot from wherever the ball ends up, which will probably be on the other side of the room!

'GET IT ROUND THE DOOR'

Make one of your holes link from one room to another. Leave the door between the rooms slightly open – about 20 centimetres or so. Try to get the ball through the gap without touching the door or doorframe.

THE 'FOIL'

Take a long sheet of aluminium foil, at least 60 centimetres wide, and crinkle it. Tape all the edges down to the floor. You must putt over this to get to a hole. The fun is that the crinkles will set the ball on a crazy path that you won't be able to control.

THE 'BOX'

Cut the top off a large cardboard box and cut 'gates' on either side. Try to make sure the gates are lined up, then turn the box upside down. Now, simply knock the ball through both gates – it's not as easy as you think!

THE 'BLINDFOLD'

Line up your shot. Then ask a friend to tie a handkerchief over your eyes – make sure you can't see through it. Now, try to make your shot.

TIPS FOR KEEPING IT SAFE AND FUN

Now you've designed your course, you are ready to begin your golf tournament. First, make sure you hide anything that could break – you don't want to destroy your mum's favourite vase, do you?

As you play, you'll think of new ideas for targets and hazards. You may find that what you've done isn't challenging enough, or there are so many hazards that it's nearly impossible. Don't be afraid to keep changing your course to improve it.

RULES

Before you start, agree the rules with your friends. That way, everyone is clear on what's allowed and what isn't – it will help avoid arguments later on. Here are some suggestions:
• You are not allowed to pick the ball up and move it.
• If you hit a bad shot you are not allowed any 'do-overs' (which means taking the shot again).
• If your ball lands in something that you can't get it out of, you can pick it up and place it back where you originally hit from and get one penalty point.
• You must not hit a person or pet with the ball or club. If you do, you are immediately out of the game.

SCORING

Keep a note of how many hits it takes for every player to get the ball into each hole. A penalty point is scored when hazards are missed or knocked over. Once all the players have completed the course, work out the winner by adding each player's penalty points to the number of times they hit the ball. The winner is the player with the fewest points at the end of the course.

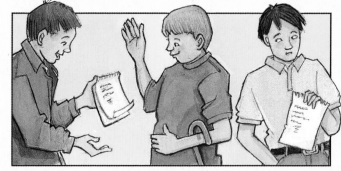

REALLY MINIATURE GOLF

If you don't have a lot of space, try building a golf course on a table top. Instead of a ball, use a marble. Your club can be a pencil or even your fingernail.

GET OFF THE COUCH,
YOU POTATO!

Tired of being a couch potato? Then here are some great ways to keep you active and fit, while having a brilliant time with your friends.

OBSTACLE COURSE

You don't need much space for this game, but it is best played outdoors.

You will need: a plastic beaker and bucket for each person / an outside tap or hose / a garden table / a deckchair / a plank of wood balanced on some bricks or a log / a bamboo cane / a football

First set up your obstacle course. You could include the following instructions: walk backwards around the garden table / do a star-jump / run five times around the deckchair / walk along the balancing plank / jump over a bamboo cane five times / hop up and down on one foot ten times / do five 'keepie-uppies' with a football and finally balance the beaker on your head for four seconds. Each player should fill their beaker with water then complete the obstacle course and empty the contents of their beaker into their bucket, before starting the whole thing again. The winner is the first person to completely fill their bucket.

To make the game harder, tell the players they can't cover their beakers with their hands.

DIZZY RUNNING

If you like a challenge, then this game is for you.

You will need: a large, flat grassy area in a park or garden / cushions or other soft items in case you fall / a walking stick or a stick of similar length

First, place the cushions or other soft items in a straight line with a metre between each one. This is your course. Now, stand at the start of the course and hold the stick to your chest. The top should be roughly 30 centimetres above your head.

Look up at the top of the stick and spin around five times, as fast as you can. Ask your friends to count out loud as you go. Stop and drop the stick, then try your best to weave in and out of the cushions along the course, as quickly as possible. Your goal is to reach the end of the course without touching any of the cushions, then turn around and head back to the start. Good luck!

JOKE TIME

SEVENS

This game can be played alone or with friends. The level of difficulty increases as you go along.

You will need: a wall / a ball that bounces / some tarmac or other level ground, which should be well swept, so that it's free of pebbles.

Start by standing roughly 2 metres from the wall then follow this sequence of instructions. It doesn't matter if you throw the ball under or over arm.

1. Bounce the ball against the wall and catch it.
2. Bounce the ball against the wall, let it hit the ground once and catch it.
3. Bounce the ball against the wall, hit it back at the wall with the palm of your hand and catch it.
4. Bounce the ball against the wall, hit it back at the wall, let it hit the ground once and catch it.
5. Bounce the ball against the wall, let it hit the ground once, bounce it on the ground again with your hand and catch it.
6. Bounce the ball against the wall, hit it back at the wall and let it hit the ground once, bounce it on the ground again and catch it.
7. Bounce the ball against the wall, hit it back at the wall and let it hit the ground once, bounce it on the ground, hit it back at the wall and catch it.

Once you know these steps inside out it's time to add extra challenges. Each time you repeat the sequence add in one of the following instructions:

• Clap your hands once after throwing the ball.
• Spin around each time you throw the ball.
• Go through each step using only your right hand and then only your left hand.
• Start each step by throwing the ball under your left leg, then repeat using your right leg.

• THE MISSING •
SUIT OF ARMOUR

Frankie Stein and his girlfriend, Edna, are going to a fancy dress party this evening.
Frankie is going as a knight – but he has lost all the pieces of his armour.
Frankie's friends have 'borrowed' them and put the pieces to good, but unusual use!
Can you spot all the missing items and get Frankie ready in time? The answers are on page 61.

Do you think you spotted all of Frankie's missing armour? Here's a checklist for you…

helmet x1 ☐

arm pieces x2 ☐

breastplate x1 ☐

shield x1 ☐

gauntlets x2 ☐

sword x1 ☐

leg pieces x2 ☐

lance x1 ☐

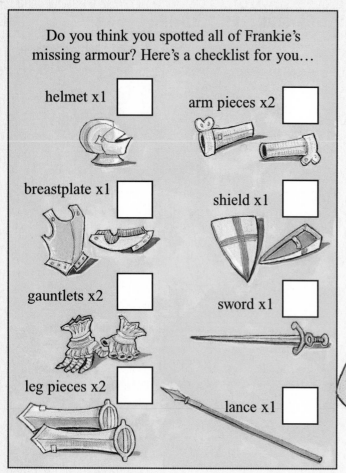

BACK AT FRANKIE STEIN'S HOUSE…

OH, FELLAS! YOU'VE FOUND IT! THANKS.

SURPRISE!

A MONSTER PARTY

Frankie's friends returned all the armour pieces just in time and all came to the party in fancy dress, too! Can you spot the ten differences between these two pictures?

MINIBEAST MONSTERS

It's sometimes hard to imagine Mother Nature having a dark side, but she does! Here are some gruesome facts about the minibeast world.

AMAZON ANTS

Amazon ants have a cruel way of capturing large prey, and they don't put it out of its misery quickly. They make a trap from plant hair fibres. When their victim walks over the hairs its legs fall through the holes. The ants then pull on the legs, stretching them, as if they were on a Medieval torture rack, before stinging them to death.

SLUGS

The biggest slug in the world is called limax cinereoniger, sometimes known as the ash-black slug. It can reach an amazing length of 30 centimetres.

CENTIPEDES

Centipedes have jaws that inject their prey with poison, paralysing it before eating it.

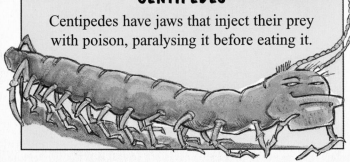

SPIDERS

Everyone knows that some spiders catch their prey in webs, but do you know what they do with their victim once they've caught it? First, a spider uses its fangs to inject a poison that paralyses its prey, then it wraps it in silk and waits for it to die. Next the spider vomits over the prey, which causes its body tissues and organs to liquefy. The spider can then suck up the liquefied tissue – slurping it up like a buggy cocktail. It gets rid of any hard bits that are hard to digest in a little ball.

ASSASSIN BUGS

There is a family of bugs called 'assassin bugs', known for their killing characteristics. One of the most famous is the wheel bug. The wheel bug's sharp straw-like mouthpiece first pierces its victim and then liquefies the insides, ending up with a tasty, insect smoothie treat!

MINIBEAST PUZZLES

Here are some minibeast puzzles for you to try. All answers can be found on page 61.

MASSES OF MAGGOTS

Maggots enjoy eating. On which piece of food are the most maggots feasting?

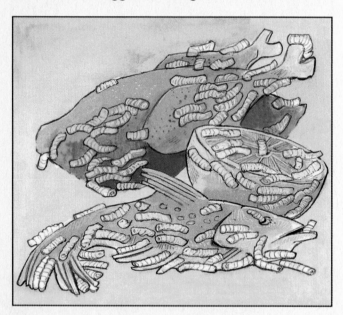

TRAPPED – HELP!

This Amazon ant has captured lots of prey. Which three pictures below are from the main image?

MINIBEAST TRUE OR FALSE

How much do you really know about minibeasts? Are these facts true or false?

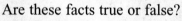

1. Maggots will eat any kind of flesh, either on a dead or living body.
2. All spiders spin webs.
3. A spider's web the size of a football field was found in Texas.
4. Some cockroaches hiss.
5. In Thailand, you can eat grilled tarantula.
6. Cockroaches are dirty creatures.
7. Having cockroaches in the house can cause asthma in children.
8. Assassin bugs are great to keep as pets.
9. Maggots glow in the dark.
10. Slugs can grow as long as 30 centimetres.

TERMITES

In a colony of termites, one termite is known as the queen. She can live for up to 25 years and lay as many as 60,000 eggs during her lifetime.

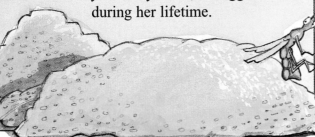

SCORPIONS

Scorpion mothers carry their young on their backs for protection. However, if the baby isn't careful and gets in front of the mother, it can get eaten.

TACHINID FLIES

Tachinid flies come in hundreds of varieties, but most have the same thing in common – the mother fly lays her eggs in, on or near a living host, such as a caterpillar or a moth. That host is then used as food for the fly's larvae once they have hatched. The larvae begin to devour the host, eating it from the inside out, until they are fully-formed and ready to fly off.

COCKROACHES

In the cockroach world, it's not the other bugs you've got to look out for, it's your best mate! Cockroaches are cannibalistic – this means they think nothing of eating dead or dying cockroach friends and relatives. If that's not bad enough, they'll happily follow it down with the poo of other cockroaches for pudding.

SLAVE-RAIDING ANTS

Over time, slave-raiding ants have lost the ability to do many of the things that are necessary to keep them alive, such as feeding themselves or looking after their young. All they can do is fight. So they have developed a somewhat cruel and sneaky solution – they steal the larvae of other species of ants and enslave them to do all the work for them. The new ants, knowing nothing different, spend their lives nursing, feeding and serving their masters.

MAGGOTS

The world would be full of the gooey, rotting, stinking flesh of dead animals and rubbish, if it wasn't for these incredible eaters. A maggot is an eating machine – little more than a mouth, a gut and a muscle.

MORE CARTOON CRAZINESS

These figures are called stick men. They are perfect when you want to draw cartoons showing action and movement.

BACK TO BASICS

Most cartoonists start their pictures by drawing stick people. It helps them to get the proportions of a human body just right.

You can make stick people as simple or as complicated as you like.

STICK PERSON 1

Drawing a stick man like this is a perfect way of working out the proportion of the human body.

STICK PERSON 2

Draw a stick man and break your lines where there are joints. This is great for shaping the arms, legs and body.

STICK PERSON 3

Draw a stick man with lines for hips and shoulders and your figure willl start to look more human.

POSING PERSONS

Getting the pose of your figure just right will come more easily if you have got your proportions worked out.

The poses below show how expressive a stick person can be.

FLESHING OUT

1. To develop your stick figures it is important to know what a real human skeleton looks like. This picture shows two views of a human skeleton.

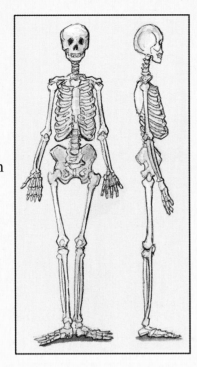

Now you can take the main components and make them simpler, as shown in the picture below. Don't forget, the figures you draw will eventually be covered by clothes, so don't get stuck on lots of detail. The red areas on this picture show the main joints – wrist, elbow, etc. These are the 'turning points' of the body.

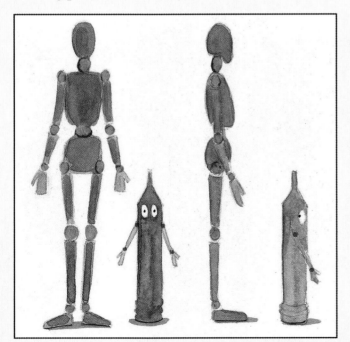

Now it's time to add some bulk to your person. Add simple shapes – squares, oblongs, ovals and circles, even triangles – to flesh it out. You must decide which works best for each part of the body.

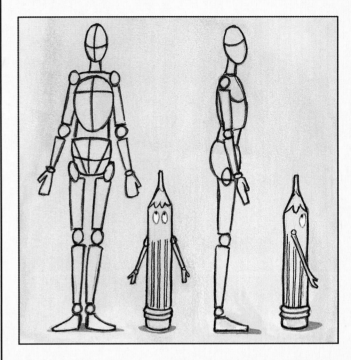

Below are some basic poses. See if you can create some of your own using what you have found out on these pages.

JOKE TIME

Q. What are two things you cannot have for breakfast?
A. Lunch and dinner!

TRY DIFFERENT SIZES

Now it's time to try making your
people tall, short, fat and thin.

HANDS AND FEET

The best way to tackle hands and feet is by starting with some basic lines
and adding on the flesh using oblongs and circles, as before.

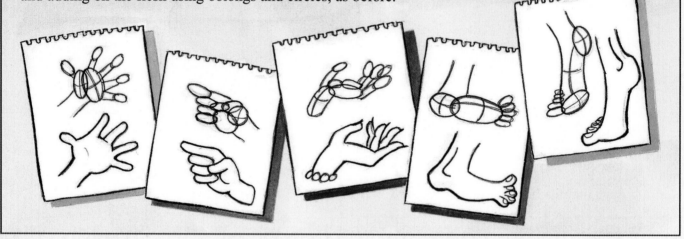

FACES

Facial expressions are essential
to show what a character is
meant to be feeling. The way
you draw the face can also
affect whether it looks realistic
or more stylized – it depends
what you want.

Here are just a couple of
different styles to try.

Even if you think you aren't
very good at first, keep
trying. You'll improve
in no time at all.

AMAZING BOYS!

Most boys are happy just to hang out with their friends, but not these boys. These boys looked at things that were wrong with the world and decided to do something about it.

THE BOY WHO BUILT A SCHOOL

Austin Gutwein from the USA was nine years old when he watched a video about AIDS and Africa and how millions of children were losing their parents to this disease. Austin wanted to help, so he put together a 'Hoop-a-thon' for World AIDS Day. He shot 2,057 free throws to represent the 2,057 children who would become orphans during that day. People sponsored Austin and he raised £1,500. He gave the money to a children's charity called World Vision.

Since he began his project, it has become a movement across the USA called 'Hoops of Hope'. Through countrywide Hoop-a-thons and fund-raising, his organisation has already raised well over £50,000. And together with World Vision, they have helped orphaned children gain access to food, clothing, shelter, a new school and a medical testing facility.

THE YOUNGEST FUNDRAISER

When a massive earthquake hit Gujarat, in India, in 2001, four-year-old Bilaal Rajan from Toronto, Canada, was inspired to raise money to help by selling clementines to his neighbours – he raised over $350.

And when the tsunami hit Southeast Asia in 2004 Bilaal encouraged children all over Canada to try to raise $100 each to help, with a total goal of $1 million. Aged eight, he raised $50,000 for the victims himself. The Toronto School Board was so impressed they contributed $1.3 million to the campaign and the Canadian Government brought the grand total to an incredible $4 million!

Bilaal speaks all over the world to help raise money and awareness and is now the National Child Representative for UNICEF in Canada (United Nations Children's Fund).

ANSWERS

YO, HO, HO!

FLAG MATCH (page 14)

The flag that has an exact pair is C – the one flown by Black Bart.

LIE OR TRUTH? (page 14)

You must ask a question to which you know the answer. The two pirates would answer differently.

For example, if you asked both pirates, 'Are you a girl?' The pirate who lies would answer 'yes'. The pirate who always tells the truth would answer that same question, 'no'.

PIRATE RIDDLES (page 14)

1. = a parrot
2. = a wooden leg
3. = the sea
4. = treasure

AHOY THERE, ME HEARTIES! (page 15)

2. There are 6 parrots.
4. The British ship has the major leak.

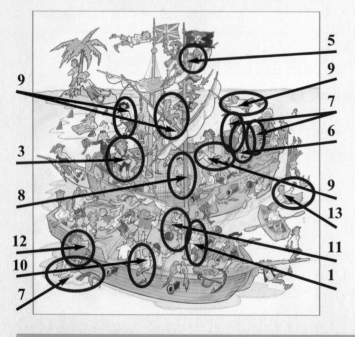

A BOY PHARAOH AND...

THE GREAT PYRAMID MAZE (page 29)

IT'S ALL EGYPTIAN TO ME

THE GOD GUESSING GAME (page 30)

1. = G 2. = D 3. = B 4. = C 5. = F
6. = A 7. = I 8. = J 9. = H 10. = E

HIEROGLYPHS (page 31)

The sentence reads: King Tut's mummy wants his teddy bear

PUZZLES AND PARASITES

TRUE OR FALSE (page 36)

1. False. They come out of your bottom! 2. True.
3. True. Doctors put them on wounds to eat the dead, infected flesh and keep the soldier infection-free. 4. True. 5. False. Bubonic plague cases can still be found around the world. However, it usually affects animals. 6. False. They only spread through contact, so usually by sharing a comb, or a hat.
7. False: Nits start biting 7-10 days after hatching.
8. False. Although some of the most dramatic ones that affect humans are in tropical countries, they are found in most parts of the world.

JOKE TIME

Q. What's the cure for flat feet?
A. A foot pump!

JOKE TIME

Knock, Knock!
Who's there?
Dismay.
Dismay who?
Dis-may be the wrong door!

THE LIFE CYCLE OF HEAD LICE (page 36)

The correct order should be: G, A, D, B, F, E, H, C

FLEAS (page 37)

There are 38 fleas on the boy's scalp.

CANINE KILLER (page 37)

Path B will lead Rover to his monthly pill.

THE MISSING SUIT OF ARMOUR (pages 50 – 52)

A MONSTER PARTY (page 52)

MINIBEAST PUZZLES

MASSES OF MAGGOTS (page 54)

There are more maggots feasting on the chicken.

MINIBEAST TRUE OR FALSE (page 54)

1. False. Maggots only eat dead flesh or infected tissue. **2.** False. Some spiders, such as the wolf spider, simply chase and attack their victim.
3. True. **4.** True. The giant hissing cockroach of Madagascar makes a hissing noise if it's disturbed, or angry. **5.** True. **6.** False. Like most insects, cockroaches keep themselves very clean.
7. True. **8.** False. People do keep them as pets, but they have the most painful bite in the bug world and can give you serious diseases. **9.** True.
10. True.

TRAPPED – HELP! (page 54)

Boxes B, C and H can be found in the main picture.